BECOMING THE PANNELL WITCH

A PREQUEL

MELISSA MANNERS

MELISSA MANNERS PUBLISHING

1

DINNER

Kippax, West Yorkshire, 1556

Mary chopped the carrots in front of her and ran over the words in her mind. She wanted to be ready to explain to her father exactly why she was ready to look for work.

'Put the pot of potatoes over the fire,' Mary told Ellen, pointing to the glimmering flames in the middle of the room.

Ellen was fourteen now, old enough to be cooking for the family. She sighed. 'Can't you do it? I'm waiting for someone.' She was kneeling on the bench by the window, eyes fixed on the path that led up to their door.

Mary put the water on to boil herself and narrowed her eyes. 'Who are you expecting? Have you invited over a guest? Did you ask Father's permission?' She didn't want one of Ellen's friends coming round and spoiling her chance to speak to him. He didn't often join them for dinner, and he was in a good mood today, so it was the perfect opportunity.

'Don't worry, he knows,' she giggled.

She added the carrots and once they were soft, she dished them out onto plates. Then she took the chicken out of the oven and used a sharp knife to carve it for them.

Ellen shrieked and ran over to look out of the window.

'Will you keep it down?' Mary asked.

'He's here,' Ellen said.

A tall, slender man with a head full of dark hair was heading towards their small house.

'Father? Are we having a guest for dinner?'

Their father emerged from his room yawning.

'Father?' Mary repeated.

He rubbed his eyes, just woken from a nap. 'Well yes, young John Pannell will be joining us this evening. Didn't I say?'

Mary tutted. 'No, you didn't. I'll serve up another plate.' There weren't quite enough potatoes left, so she picked one off each of their plates and added to the last one. 'Ellen, set out the tablecloth, and bring the extra chair from outside. Oh, and go and fetch us some wine.'

She grinned, and this time did as she was asked without arguing.

'Father, you can't greet a guest like this—go and put a shirt on. And comb your hair.' He raised his eyebrows but did as Mary told him. His head was mostly bald, but his grey hair stuck up in the air like he had just been running around in the wind.

Mary combed her own hair and had just enough time to change her dress before she heard the knock on the door. Mary stepped into the main room with a deep breath.

Her father invited the man inside and introduced him to his youngest daughter, Ellen. 'You know my son, William, of course—he's working tonight. And this is my eldest, Mary,' he said with a wide smile.

He couldn't have been older than twenty. His silky hair was pushed back, emphasising his high cheekbones and broad jawline. He was clean shaven and wore undamaged, uncreased clothes. None of the men in town took care of themselves like this. 'Pleased to meet you.' He gave a slight bow of his head. 'Let me see you.'

Mary stood up straight, hands held behind her back, eyes on the ground.

Ellen smirked. 'Turn around, then! And do it slowly.'

Mary's cheeks burned, but she took hold of her skirts and twirled in a small circle.

'You'll do just fine.' He ran his eyes over her, then spoke to her father. 'She's not too plain, not too thin. In fact, she could even be considered beautiful.'

Ellen gasped.

Her father grinned. 'Like her mother.'

He went on, 'I'm John Pannell. I actually grew up in Kippax but I've been away for a number of years, working. You don't need to know about all of that.' His voice was deep and smooth.

There was no denying that he was an attractive man, but so far, everything he had said made her uncomfortable. She smiled politely. 'Thank you for joining us. Please, sit down,' Mary gestured to the table, where her family were already sitting. Ellen was sitting in the garden chair—she had left her normal seat, next to Mary's, for John.

Mary brought over the plates, serving John first and herself last.

John stood and pulled out Mary's chair for her to sit down, brushing her shoulder as he tucked her under the table. Mary wasn't sure if it was on purpose, but his touch made her shiver.

Their father thanked God for their food before they ate. 'It's good to see you again, John. How's your mother?'

John finished chewing and wiped the corners of his mouth before answering. 'She's better, thank you. Still misses my father, of course. But glad to have me back in town, I think.'

He grinned. 'Good to hear.' He addressed his children. 'I knew John's father as a boy, you know. We worked together for years before he had the accident.'

Mary knew what he was talking about. A few years ago, there was a mining explosion which killed a lot of the men in Kippax. Mary's father worked on the farms and was one of the men called to the search and rescue operation, but the mine had collapsed, burying most of the miners underground. Afterwards, a lot of young sons were sent to the mines in their father's place to support their families. They were lucky their father hadn't been a miner—they would have had nobody else to look after them. John didn't seem too affected by it now, but Mary knew exactly what it was like to lose a parent, regardless of how much you might hide your feelings.

'Yes, it was my mother who suggested I look you up, actually.' John gazed at Mary, though he was talking to her father. Then he added, 'the food is delicious, by the way. Almost as good as that of a professional cook.'

Mary knew she was better than that—she had always excelled in the kitchen. But she didn't want to be rude to a guest, so she bit her tongue. 'Thank you.'

Her father gleamed with pride. 'She'll make a great wife one day.'

'Not for a while, I'm sure,' Mary added, avoiding his gaze.

Her father almost said something but John held up a hand. 'Of course. Not until the right man presents himself.'

Mary let out a breath, relieved. She returned to her dinner.

'She's done such a good job taking care of Ellen all these years, and William too. She'll be a great mother,' her father added.

Mary's jaw tensed up again.

John shook his head. 'It's nothing for you to worry about. Women love motherhood, trust me. I'm sure you'll take to it quite easily.'

How could he be so confident about how she would feel? She looked sideways at his big green eyes. It was difficult to work him out. 'Are you looking to get married soon?'

Ellen hadn't eaten a bite of her dinner. Instead her eyes were glued to her sister and John, desperate to hear their conversation.

'Who doesn't want to fall in love?' He locked eyes with her. Despite his behaviour, he did seem to like her. He hadn't looked at anyone else since he arrived.

Mary's father cleared his throat loudly, making Mary jump.

'Oh!' She ran her eyes around the table. 'I'm sorry. Are you all finished?' She piled up the plates and took them away, before refilling the wine cups.

'Ellen? I need to talk to you. Come outside for a minute,' their father said.

Mary's eyes widened.

As soon as they were alone, John took her hand in his. 'You should know, I'm planning to ask your father for your hand.'

Mary took a deep breath in.

He scooted his chair closer to hers and reached over to whisper in her ear. 'There's something between us. I know you feel it too. Say you'll marry me.'

The hairs on the back of her neck stood on end. She hadn't realised he was going to propose—at least not tonight. They had only just met, and she knew almost nothing about him or his family. She wanted to explain this to him and ask why he was asking so soon. Maybe they could discuss it and he would see what an unreasonable request this was. But the words didn't come out. Instead, she whispered, her voice shaking, 'but we're so young.'

'We don't have to marry right away, if that's what you're worried about. I'll happily wait days, even weeks, for your hand.'

Mary bit her lip, not sure how to respond.

John kissed her hand before releasing it, searching her eyes for an answer. It didn't come, but still he went outside to speak to her father.

When John left, her father came back in with a wide grin on his face. 'I think we all know what happens next.'

Ellen slumped down at the table.

'Now I suppose you'll want weeks to plan the wedding? And money, too. Hmm.'

'When will I get our room to myself?' Ellen added.

'I'll need to have a word with the priest,' their father mumbled.

'Stop!' Mary cried.

The room fell into silence.

'I can't marry him.'

Her father glared at her. 'Out,' he ordered Ellen. She hurried outside, shutting the door behind her, though Ellen's hair was visible by the window—she was still listening.

'I want what's best for you,' he started. 'You know that don't you?'

Mary nodded.

'Haven't I always been good to you?'

It was true, he was a good father. They had sometimes struggled financially, but what family didn't? He never laid a hand on them, and he never forced them to accept a stepmother they hated. Mary didn't want him to be offended. She whispered, 'please. Don't make me marry him.'

He shook his head. 'Make you marry him? Didn't I see how well the two of you got on? He's young, handsome and has the means to support you. He has even agreed to take care of your brother and sister, should I die before they can take care of themselves. What could you have against that?'

'Nothing. It's not that. I like him, really I do. But I thought now that I'm eighteen, I could finally have some freedom. Ellen and William could pitch in around the house. I could stop doing everything around here.'

'Everything?' He raised his voice. 'You say you do everything around here?' He stood and paced from one side of the room to the other. 'Do you realise how much I've sacrificed for this family? How many men do you know who raised a family on their own? Ever since your mother died, I've done whatever it takes to keep this family going. How could you have the audacity to walk away from us now?'

Mary shook her head vigorously. 'No, Father. It's not that. I'm truly grateful for you. I just need some time—'

He interrupted her. 'Time? No. I won't accept it. You've put off marriage for years, but you can't keep it up forever. Girls marry. That's all there is to it.'

'Not everyone marries,' she muttered.

He took her hand. 'My dear, don't be nervous. There's no reason you shouldn't be married. You're a fine-looking girl with good manners. Why shouldn't John want to marry you?'

'It's not that.'

'What then?'

'Just because it's the normal thing to do, it doesn't mean I should have to do it.'

He sighed. 'There's nothing wrong with the man, and I know you like him. It doesn't have to be immediate, but within a matter of weeks, you'll marry him.'

'Father!'

'I mean it.'

Mary tried to stop the tears from falling but it was too late. 'I won't let you force me to marry.'

'You know it's best for everyone.'

'Please.' Mary dropped to her knees and reached for her father's hands. 'I'm begging you, don't make me do this. Don't punish me. It's not my fault Mother died. I should have never had to take up all her responsibilities so young. All these years I've been stuck here.'

He brushed her hands away. 'Stuck? Stuck with your family?'

Mary knew she shouldn't have said that, but it was too late.

'If that's how you feel, you can sleep somewhere else tonight.'

'But Father—'

'Get out, now.'

2

THE CHAPMANS

The Chapmans, Thomas and John, had wanted a maid for years, but always claimed they couldn't afford one. Mary put her case to them: she would run their house as it should be run, even living there to make sure it was clean and they always had food cooked for them. To prove her worth, she worked her first few days for free, which was enough to convince Thomas they needed her.

It was during her first week there that it happened. She awoke early after tossing and turning on her pallet next to the kitchen fire. Starting with lighting the fires, she then dusted the rooms and swept the floors before preparing some food for the family.

She knocked for Thomas. He groaned as usual and mumbled something unintelligible, so she called, 'breakfast!' and walked along the corridor to his son's bedroom. John was the same age as Mary but acted much older. He felt entitled to more than others because he was born a Chapman. It was clear to Mary that anyone in service worked much harder than him.

John said nothing when she knocked, so she pushed open the door. An open glass bottle lay horizontally on the floor. Mary hurried to pick it up, but most of the liquid had been wasted. She gave it a sniff. Whisky. John was a troubled young man with too much time and money on his hands. Mary was sure he would do better with a wife, or at least a job.

'John?' She scolded herself at the mistake and corrected herself immediately. 'Master Chapman?' He rolled over and she gasped. Her cheeks burned red. She threw a blanket over him to cover his body and shouted, 'breakfast!' Was this what it was going to be like, working in a house with two men and no women?

While they ate, she took the chance to have a quick wash. She worked long hours, but she didn't mind. For her, finally able to support herself financially, this was freedom. She ran a comb through her hair and removed her clothes. Then she dipped a cloth into a bucket of cold water. It was at this moment that she heard footsteps coming towards the kitchen door from outside. Mary peeked out of the small window and let out an involuntary squeal. A woman was heading in her direction. She reached for her clothes to cover herself before the woman could reach the door. Pulling on her blouse, the image of the woman stuck in her mind. She was tall and had wide shoulders. Her walk was confident, her back straight and she was swinging her arms by her sides. She wore no cap, and her short messy hair, light brown, shone in the sunlight in a way Mary's own dark hair never did. It was blowing about in the wind, but that didn't seem to bother her. Grown women never let their hair loose—not that Mary had ever seen, anyway. Her jawline was prominent and, combined with her high cheekbones, made her seem slightly older than Mary. Mary smoothed out the creases in her skirt and peeked outside again, to see the woman almost at the door.

Without knowing why, Mary ducked, hiding. A shiny metal pan showed her reflection. She frowned. Pinching her cheeks gave them a bit of colour. She pulled a couple of strands of hair out from under her cap. She curled one side of her mouth upwards into a smile and immediately shook her head. No. That looked silly. She tried again, this time smiling with her mouth closed and chin up in the air. No, that was wrong too. She tried a smile with her teeth showing.

The woman knocked, two hard raps, at the door.

It made Mary jump. She took a deep breath, stood up and opened the door.

'Y-yes? H-how may I help you?'

'Pleased to make your acquaintance. Elizabeth Pannell.' She spoke with the same confidence that she exuded as she walked.

Mary cleared her throat and tried to stop herself from blushing. What was wrong with her today? 'Yes. Me too. I mean, yours. I'm pleased to make your acquaintance.' Why was she so nervous? 'Good evening, Miss Pannell.' Mary said. She wondered if she was related to John—they had the same bright green eyes.

Elizabeth looked at her, waiting.

'Oh! I'm sorry. Mary. My name is Mary Tailor.'

Elizabeth smiled. 'I wonder if I might come in?'

Mary nodded, a little too quickly. Then she backed into a pile of pans which all fell to the floor with a crash. She reached to try to stop them from falling but instead knocked John's leftover porridge from the morning all down her skirt. Her cheeks burned in embarrassment.

'Oh! I apologise, I didn't mean to...' Mary trailed off and looked around frantically for something to clean up. Unfazed, Elizabeth grabbed a cloth, knelt on the floor and began to dab Mary's skirt clean.

'There.' Elizabeth wiped off all of the porridge and stood up straight. 'Miss Tailor, please, are you alright? Was that hot? Allow me. I didn't mean to disturb you.' Elizabeth motioned for Mary to sit down while she picked up the pans. When she was done, she caught her eye, but didn't say anything. It was Mary who broke the silence.

'I'm sorry—I'm so clumsy. I only got this job last week and I cannot have them let me go.'

Elizabeth smiled. 'We'll say nothing more about it. I'm here to fix a few things for my uncle—Mr Chapman. I believe I am expected?'

'Oh!' Mary let out a breath. 'I'm sorry, I was expecting a boy!'

She smirked. 'Don't be, most people would. But I'm good at this sort of thing.' Then she added, 'even though it's not normal, you know, for a woman.'

'Mr Chapman is still eating, so he won't be able to see you yet.' Mary blushed. 'Anyway, who's to say what's normal for a woman?'

Elizabeth looked Mary up and down, a curious glint in her eye. 'May I sit?'

'Please do.' Mary sat next to her, but the bench was barely big enough for one person, so their thighs were pressed against each other.

'I haven't seen you around town—where did you work before here?'

'Well, I don't know if I'd call it work, but just at home. I never had time to go out much.' She paused, trying to decide how much to share with Elizabeth. Something in her tilted expression and half smile made her think she could trust her. 'Ever since my mother died, my siblings needed me to step in.'

Elizabeth nodded. 'I'm sorry. Do you remember her?'

'No, I was only four.'

'Four? And you're the oldest?'

'It's not as bad as it sounds. We had friends and neighbours helping out for a couple of years. We didn't struggle too much.'

Elizabeth tilted her head to the side, searching Mary's eyes to see if she believed her. 'If you say so. How many siblings did you have?'

'Two brothers and a sister.' Mary took a deep breath. 'But one of my brothers died when he was a boy. So it's just the three of us and Father, now.'

'They're lucky to have you.' Elizabeth squeezed her hand.

Mary smiled. 'Thanks. What's your family like?'

'It's just the two of us—I don't know what I'd do without my mother. She's all I have.'

'Are you close?'

'Very close. We always have been. Mother Pannell might not have given birth to me, but that doesn't make her any less my mother. If anything, she's more than that. She fought to keep me. Plenty of mothers don't fight for their children how she fought for me.' Elizabeth stood up and leaned against the kitchen counter.

Mary repeated the name in her mind. Mother Pannell. She had heard it before, from her father. John Pannell was distantly related to her. 'Is that the same Mother Pannell that saved our town from the plague all those years ago?'

'That's what they say.'

'I didn't even know she was still alive. She originally came to Kippax to get married, didn't she?'

Elizabeth nodded.

'But she doesn't have a husband now?'

'No, he died years ago. Right around the time I was born.'

'What were your parents like?'

Elizabeth hesitated. 'I never knew my mother or my father. Mother Pannell took me in as a baby.'

Mary wanted to ask why. She wanted to know what happened to her parents and who they were to Mother Pannell that meant she was the one who took her in. 'It's fine—we don't need to keep talking about it.'

Elizabeth's shoulders relaxed. She gestured around them, to the house. 'So what brings you here, to the Chapmans?'

Mary stood up and started to tidy away some of the plates she had put out to dry earlier. 'I'm good at this. I've been running our household for years. It made sense to take a job here.'

'Was it your father who suggested you look for work?' Elizabeth picked up a rag and helped her to dry up.

'Actually, no.' Mary bit her lip.

'I'm sorry if it's too personal—you don't have to say if you don't want to.' Her fingers brushed against Mary's and it sent sparks through her whole body. Her cheeks burned red. She found her attractive, like she did John, but Elizabeth seemed caring and thoughtful in a way that John would never be.

'I don't mind,' she said, her voice wobbling. 'No, he didn't want me to work at all. He tried to make me get married to his friend's son, John.'

They finished up and Elizabeth took the rags and put them in the pile of dirty linens. She looked into Mary's eyes. 'You don't love him?'

Mary didn't take her eyes off her. 'It's not that,' she started. 'I just don't know him yet. We've only just met.' It struck Mary that she had only just met Elizabeth, and already they were sharing much more than she had felt able to share with John. 'Anyway, why should I have to get married? Just because I'm old enough?

Just because my family don't need me anymore? I should get a choice in my own life.'

'You should!'

'I've looked after my family for years, and all I wanted was the chance to decide what to do next, on my own. I'm happy to work, I just want to live on my own terms.'

Elizabeth grinned and squeezed Mary's hand more tightly. 'You're so passionate.'

Mary blushed.

'It's a good thing. I wish I felt that strongly about something.'

'Don't you have something you want to do with your life?'

Elizabeth shrugged. 'I suppose I'd like the chance to read more widely. You know, learn all those things well-born boys get taught.'

'I can't think of anything worse,' Mary smirked.

'It just seems like there's so much more to learn. About the world, about the people in it. I'd love to read about it.'

'If that's what you want to do, I'm sure you'll find a way.'

Elizabeth kept hold of Mary's gaze, her face only inches from hers.

Mary's heart felt like it was going to beat out of her chest. For one crazy moment, she thought Elizabeth was going to kiss her.

But right then, the door swung open.

They stood and stepped immediately apart from each other.

The man standing in the doorway with a look of horror on his face was Mary's father. 'What are you doing?'

Mary kept her eyes on the floor, blinking to try to stop her tears from falling.

He shook his head. 'I don't believe this. Were you two just—?'

Elizabeth mouthed, 'I'm sorry, I need to get to work,' and backed out of the kitchen door to go and find Mr Chapman.

Mary sobbed. 'Please, Father. It's not what you think.'

He made a face. 'Is she the real reason you won't marry John?'

'No!' Mary reached for his hand but he pulled away. 'This isn't about her. I only just met her; she was only comforting me.'

'I saw what you were doing. Don't come back home.' He swept out of the house, leaving Mary crying on the floor.

3

MOTHER PANNELL

Mary didn't get any work done for the rest of the day. She didn't eat, she didn't clean, she didn't move. The sun went down and the kitchen was dark before anyone found her.

It was Elizabeth who came to check on her in the evening. Her face fell when she came in and found Mary crying on the floor. She knelt down and pulled her into her arms. 'Don't cry,' she whispered. 'You'll work this out.'

Mary let herself cry on Elizabeth's chest, wetting the rough linen of her shirt. Elizabeth didn't ask any questions and didn't tell her to stop. She gently stroked Mary's back and kept her close until Mary's sobs subsided. 'Thanks,' Mary said. 'I'm sorry. You don't even know me. Don't feel like you have to stay here with me.'

'I don't mind. Do you want to talk about it?'

Mary sighed and pulled away. 'There's nothing to talk about. My father made his feelings perfectly clear. I can't go home.'

'If you're worried about a place to live, I can speak to the Chapmans for you. I'm sure they'd be happy for you to live here, as you're here working all hours of the day anyway.'

Mary smiled. 'Thank you, but they've already said I can stay here.'

Elizabeth stood and held out a hand to help Mary up. 'That's good. You'll be fine, I know it.'

'I've never lived on my own before. Never had to look after myself.'

'The way I understand it, you've looked after your whole family and now it's time to focus on yourself.' Elizabeth looked into Mary's eyes with a sort of admiration that made Mary's stomach flutter.

Mary nodded. 'That's exactly what I want. Does that make me selfish?'

'No!' Elizabeth shook her head vigorously. 'It makes you human. You deserve to live your own life. I think you're right not to get married. I don't plan to.'

'Ever?'

'Ever.'

Mary raised her eyebrows. Surely Elizabeth would change her mind one day. Every woman wanted to get married, eventually, didn't they? 'Well, thank you for coming to check on me. I'm feeling better now.' She brushed some of the dust off her skirts and started to pack away some of the pots and pans that had dried earlier.

'Look, I don't want to intrude, and please don't feel obliged to say yes,' Elizabeth put a hand on Mary's shoulder, 'but would you like to join me and my mother for dinner?'

Mary's heart jumped. She really did want to spend more time with Elizabeth. 'Now?'

She grinned. 'I'm finished with work for the day if you are?'

They made their way to Mother Pannell's hut, walking side by side, Mary's hand so close to Elizabeth's that it brushed against hers. She pretended not to notice.

Once they came off the main road, they headed along a wet, muddy path towards the rural part of Kippax. Elizabeth walked a few paces ahead of Mary so that she could step where she stepped. She hoped she wouldn't slip.

'Is that it?' Mary pointed to a small wooden hut they were walking towards.

'That's it.'

When they were closer, Elizabeth peeked in through the

window, then gestured for Mary to follow her. 'She's seeing someone right now, let's go and sit by the river for a bit.'

Mary frowned. 'What do you mean, seeing someone?'

'You'll see.' She lowered herself down and sat on a dry, sloping rock, and Mary sat next to her.

'Why do you live so far away from the rest of Kippax?' Mary asked. She searched Elizabeth's eyes. She had never met anyone like her before.

'Mother likes her privacy, and so do her customers. She helps people, and although everyone knows it, it's not good to be so visible. It's easier to be out here.'

'What about you? Do you like it?'

Elizabeth smiled. 'It might not be exactly what I want—we're quite isolated out here. But I like not having to do what's expected.'

'What do you mean? What's wrong with doing what you're expected to do?' Mary frowned, suddenly defensive.

'Well, for one thing, Mother Pannell would never force me to get married.'

Elizabeth made a good point. 'What else?'

'Mother taught me to read and write.'

Mary sighed. 'I know you like it, but why? Does it ever come in handy?'

'You'd be surprised.'

Mary huffed. 'Is that all? I don't need to read or write, and I've found a way to not get married, but it doesn't mean I have to live miles away from everyone.'

Elizabeth took her hand. 'It's not about the individual things. Haven't you ever wanted the freedom to do exactly what you want, without having to worry what it looks like to others?'

Before Mary had a chance to answer, voices sounded behind them.

'Thank you, Mother Pannell. I hope it works,' the woman called.

Elizabeth dropped Mary's hand and blushed, like she'd been caught doing something.

Mother Pannell saw and her eyes locked on Mary. 'Elizabeth, in you come.'

Mary followed her inside the tiny hut, not really large enough for three adults to stand in comfortably. Mother Pannell leaned around Elizabeth to fetch a bucket of water, emptied it into a pot and placed it over the fire.

'Mother, this is Mary.'

Mother Pannell was a short, elderly woman with a long white plait that ran down her back. She had thin eyes that surveyed Mary and seemed to see right through to her soul. 'It's a pleasure to meet you,' Mary said, her voice wobbling.

'Will she be staying to eat with us?' She dropped some vegetables into the water.

'Yes.'

'Oh, fine,' she said. Her monotonous voice made it hard to tell what she was thinking.

Mary caught Elizabeth's eye and motioned to the door, trying to ask if she should leave. Elizabeth shook her head.

'Mother Pannell, do you need any help with the food?'

She raised her eyebrows. 'Are you a good cook?'

'Yes, ma'am.'

'Be my guest.' She leaned back to sit on a bench by the window while Mary took over stirring the pot.

'Who was that woman?' Elizabeth asked, sitting next to her mother.

'You know old Ledston Hall?' Mother Pannell said.

Elizabeth nodded. 'At the top of the hill?'

'That's the one.'

'It's been empty for a long time, hasn't it?'

'It has. It's expensive to run, and of course the King wanted it to be given to a family who would use it and the lands properly.'

'And?'

'They've finally let it out to the Witham family.'

'Was that the lady of the house who came to see you?'

'Precisely. She and her husband live there, together with their nine children.'

'Nine?' Mary interrupted.

Elizabeth and Mother Pannell turned to her in surprise, as if they had forgotten she was there.

'Sorry, go on,' Mary said.

Mother Pannell said in a low voice, 'she wanted to make sure she couldn't have any more children.'

Mary frowned. 'Is that possible? You can stop a woman from having children?'

She shook her head. 'Not really. That's what I told her. You can't guarantee these things. But there are ways to reduce the possibility. Restrict activity with your husband to a certain time of the month, for example.'

Mary's eyes widened. 'What else?'

'I mixed her up a tincture to take which should reduce her fertility.'

Elizabeth rolled her eyes. She looked bored already.

'And that's all you need?'

Mother Pannell hesitated. 'There's one more thing a woman can do. Here, you see this?' She reached up to the shelf above her and pulled down a piece of something soft with holes in it, no bigger than the palm of her hand. 'This is sea sponge. If you put this, you know,' she paused, 'inside, you're less likely to get pregnant.'

Mary gasped.

How was it that this woman could defy nature? She had always thought marriage meant giving up all your freedom to your husband. He could choose the course of your life; it was up to him when you had children and exactly how many you would have. But maybe this wasn't true. Mary desperately wanted children, but she wasn't ready yet. 'Fascinating,' she muttered.

Mother Pannell raised her eyebrows and addressed Elizabeth, 'where did you find this girl?'

Elizabeth grinned.

4

REMEDIES

Mother Pannell's Hut, West Yorkshire, 1559

For the next three years, Mary found excuses to visit Elizabeth and Mother Pannell as often as she could. She helped countless women with Mother Pannell's remedies, and Mary was keen to learn how to mix them by herself.

One day, Mother Pannell wanted to show Mary how to make dwale, her preferred anaesthetic. She went out to find the henbane she needed for it, and Mary found herself alone in the hut with Elizabeth. They sat cross-legged in front of the fire, holding out their hands to warm them.

'I'm so glad we met,' Elizabeth said.

'Me too.'

'Because of the work you do with Mother Pannell?' Elizabeth looked sideways at her.

Mary's cheeks flushed. 'No. Well, that's part of it. I do enjoy helping people. And her work is so interesting.'

'Then what?' Elizabeth edged closer to Mary until their knees touched.

'I—I like spending time with you,' Mary whispered.

Elizabeth pulled off Mary's cap and ran her fingers through her hair, letting the dark waves fall past her shoulders. 'You're beautiful.'

Mary's heart beat faster. Her eyes were locked onto Elizabeth's. There was no denying it—Elizabeth wanted to kiss her. She leaned in.

Too many thoughts raced around inside Mary's mind and she couldn't make sense of them. She wanted to kiss Elizabeth back, but what would that mean? She pushed her away.

'What's wrong?' Elizabeth whispered.

'I—I can't.'

5

WITCH

That evening, Mother Pannell returned to find them separate; Elizabeth was outside, tending to the garden, and Mary was inside, finishing the mixture they needed to prepare the dwale. It was rare that they weren't together. 'What's wrong with you two?'

Before they had the chance to respond, someone rapped at the door and pushed it open. It was a man. In the three years since she started working with Mother Pannell, she had only treated women. Men didn't tend to know about her remedies, let alone come to ask for them.

'I need a doctor for my wife,' he called. 'She's hurt.'

'Shh,' Mother Pannell said. 'Sit here, calm down. Tell me what happened.'

He took a deep breath and then went on, still agitated, 'it's urgent. She burned her arm. She told me to come here, said I could find a doctor here who wouldn't charge as much as normal. Where is he?'

'It's me,' Mother Pannell said. 'I can help.'

He raised his eyebrows.

'What did she burn herself on?'

'What does that matter?' The man was shouting again. 'I said, it's urgent. She's hurt.'

'Fire? Boiling water?'

'Er, yes. It was boiling water. She—she spilled it on herself.'

'Is the burn large?'

He hesitated before answering. 'It's on her arm. And shoulder.'

Mary tried to catch Mother Pannell's eye. Something wasn't right here. But she was too caught up in trying to help the poor woman. She grabbed a knife, ran out into the dark and came back in a second with a long, green leaf of some kind. 'This is called aloe vera,' she said to Mary. 'Watch how I prepare it.'

Mary watched. She wanted to learn, and Mother Pannell was happy to teach her.

'First, cut off these sharp spines at the edges.' She sliced off the sides of the leaf. 'Then, cut right through the middle, and pull the top and bottom part of the leaf away from each other.' She placed the two parts of the leaf on the table.

'What is that smell?' The man asked, holding his nose.

'Just wait, you'll have the remedy soon enough and you can be on your way. It smells, but it works.' She called to Mary, 'come, I'll do this part, you do that one. See how I'm scoring it, first in this direction, then in another?'

Mary took another knife and scored the leaf. The smell was very strong up close. There was an odd sort of clear jelly oozing out of the leaf that Mary was about to wipe away.

'No, don't do that—that's the substance we want,' Mother Pannell said. She grabbed a jar and put the leaves in it. 'Here you go, sir. If you rub these leaves on your wife's burns every couple of hours, she'll start feeling better in no time.'

He narrowed his eyes. 'That's all? I just rub this on her arm?'

'That's right. Every two hours, until she's feeling better.'

'If this doesn't work, I'll be back.'

'It will work, but if you need some more, I'll be here.'

He handed her a pile of coins and left.

'Mother Pannell, something's not right.'

'What do you mean?'

'That man—he seemed—'

'Seemed what?'

Mary stuttered over her words. 'I wouldn't want to accuse

someone without knowing them, but it sounded like he might have burned his wife on purpose.'

Mother Pannell didn't say anything.

'Did you hear what I said?'

'I heard you fine.'

'But don't you think that's what it sounded like?'

She sighed. 'I do. But what do you expect me to do about it? Kick up a fuss? Threaten him? All that would do is stop him coming to me next time she's hurt.'

'But there must be something we can do.'

'This sort of thing happens more than you might think. But it's my job to help the women of our town—that's all.'

The door banged opened again and there stood John. He shook his head at Mary, disapproving.

'John!' Mary said.

'I heard what just happened in here. I was listening at the door.'

'Mother Pannell, this is John.'

She looked him up and down and frowned. 'I know. We've met.'

Mary looked from her to him.

'What are you doing, associating with the likes of her?' John asked Mary.

She didn't know what to say.

Mother Pannell pushed him out of the doorway and stood outside with him. 'John—you may not know how things work around here, but I help the people of Kippax. I always have. You try telling anyone otherwise, it'll be you they drive away, not me!'

He gave her a one-sided smile. 'I know, old woman. I don't care about you. It's her.' He pointed into the hut at Mary, who was chopping a handful of parsley. 'Look at her! She's been practising witchcraft out here, with you, and that's why she refused to marry me. I knew it.'

'John, come on,' Mary said. He was angry, but the redness of his cheeks and the confidence of his stance only seemed to make him more attractive to her. 'You know very well I'm no witch.'

He shook his head. 'I know you want to marry me. I can see it. I'll fight for you, whatever it takes.'

Mary drew in a breath.

John went on, 'you think the people won't believe me? Do you think you'll be allowed to stay here, in this witches' hut, making potions and chanting curses?'

Mary didn't like where he was going with this. The penalty for witchcraft was hanging. 'Please, don't say anything.'

'You know what I want in return.'

Mary shook her head. 'No.'

'Marry me. I know you want to. Be my wife, give me a son and I'll keep your secret.'

'No.'

'I'll even let you keep coming here, to work, if you like it so much. Any other husband would make you stop, but not me. I'm one of the good ones.'

Mary hesitated.

'I know you want children one day. Wouldn't you rather have them with someone who knows about this side of you? Knows it and loves you despite all of it? I'll take good care of you.'

Mary did want children, more than anything.

Elizabeth had finished outside and was at the door, listening.

'Mary, don't,' she urged.

'I'm sorry.'

6

ROMANCE

Mary ran after Elizabeth, leaving John and Mother Pannell behind. 'Wait, let me explain,' she called. Mary had to pull her skirts up high so they didn't dip into the deep, wet mud. They were off the main path, headed towards the woods.

'There's nothing to explain.' Elizabeth knelt under the thick branch of an oak tree and twisted her body around the trunk. Mary struggled to follow.

'Please,' Mary tried again. 'Where are you going?'

'Go home. I want to be alone.'

Mary ignored her.

'Mary, I can hear your breathing from here. There's nothing for us to talk about. You may as well go back, start making preparations for your wedding.' Her words were cold, but her tone of voice gave her away. She spoke in a weak voice that cracked on every other word, like she was trying not to cry.

'I'm sorry.'

'Sorry for what? You've made your choice.' She turned into a clearing, made up of a large lake surrounded by tall trees. One of them had fallen over and Elizabeth sat on it like a bench.

Mary joined her. 'Please try to understand. I never wanted to hurt you.'

'Well, you did.'

'You heard John—he said he'd accuse me of witchcraft. I didn't have a choice.'

Elizabeth scoffed. 'There's always a choice. Don't pretend like part of you doesn't want to marry him.'

'Is it so bad that I want to have children? And if I'm going to marry someone, why not him? Please, don't be angry with me.'

'I'm not angry.' Her voice quietened to a whisper. 'I'm hurt. I thought there was something between us.'

Mary edged towards her on the tree trunk. 'There is.'

Elizabeth hesitated. 'But back at the hut—why did you pull away?'

'I'm sorry.' Mary bit her lip. 'I got scared. We're not supposed to be together, you and me.'

'Who says?' Elizabeth put a hand on Mary's thigh.

'I—well, no one. But we shouldn't.'

'Do you want to?' Elizabeth whispered in her ear, so quietly that it made Mary shiver.

'Yes. Yes, I really, truly want to,' Mary said.

'Come here,' Elizabeth whispered, as she pulled her closer.

Mary put a hand on Elizabeth's waist. She kept her gaze and brought her lips closer. She pressed them softly against Elizabeth's and pulled away. After a moment of hesitation, she kissed her again, firmly this time. She swung a leg over so that she was sitting on her lap.

Elizabeth's hands were on her back, pulling her closer. She moaned softly and when Mary did too, Elizabeth rolled her over and pushed her onto the muddy ground.

When they were done, Elizabeth kissed Mary's forehead softly. Mary giggled, lost in a state of bliss. All her worries from earlier had melted away.

'Let's go swimming,' Elizabeth said with a wink.

'Swimming? It's too cold!'

Elizabeth grinned. 'That's part of the fun. Come on.' She peeled off her slip, the only item of clothing she was still wearing. Then she pulled the pins out of her hair so that she could shake it free. She ran up to the bank and jumped in.

Mary took a deep breath before she followed Elizabeth into the freezing cold water. She was soon to be married, after all. Why shouldn't she enjoy today while she still could?

7

CHOICES

Mary's Father's House, West Yorkshire, 1559

Mary's father smiled weakly. 'It's good to have you back home.'

She dipped some bread into her stew and chewed on it, refusing to answer him.

'You've made the right choice, marrying John,' he tried again. 'Though you're lucky he was willing to wait for you all this time!'

'Leave her alone,' Ellen said. She was seventeen years old now, old enough to stand up to her father. 'She's doing what you all want, so give her some space.'

Mary gave her sister a weak smile.

Elizabeth's voice shouted at the door. 'Mary? Mary, let me in!'

Ellen sighed. 'Leave it to me. I'll get rid of her.' She wiped her mouth and made her way to the door. 'Hello, Elizabeth. This isn't a good time.'

'Don't do this,' she called to Mary. 'I know you don't love him.'

Mary carried on eating with her head down, tears slipping down her cheeks into her bowl.

'It's not too late. You're not married yet. Come and stay with me for a few days, take some time to think about what you want.'

Mary's father gulped down his beer and slammed the mug on

the table, before storming over to the door. 'What do you think you're doing here?'

Elizabeth stopped shouting.

'This is my house, and Mary is my daughter. Do you hear me?'

Elizabeth nodded, with gritted teeth.

'She has spent the last three years as a servant living in God knows what kind of quarters, with no hope of marriage or children. All because you've been filling her head with all sorts of nonsense. It stops here. John is a good man and he's waited for her all this time. I will not have you ruin her life.'

Mary couldn't help but turn to look at Elizabeth, whose face was bright red in anger. Her fists clenched at her sides, she pushed past Mary's father into the house. She spoke like she didn't care who listened. 'Mary, listen. Please don't do this. He won't make you happy, I know it.'

Mary cleared her throat. 'What other choice do I have?'

Elizabeth whispered so that only Mary could hear her, 'choose me.'

Mary's cheeks burned. Her family was right there, what was Elizabeth thinking? 'You can't come here and say that!' Then in a low voice, 'besides, what kind of life would we have? I want children, you know that. I'm not like you. Marriage isn't something you want for yourself, but I've always seen myself as a wife, and more importantly, a mother. It's the normal thing to do.' It was like Mary could hear her father saying the words through her.

Tears started to form in Elizabeth's eyes. Mary had never seen her cry. 'Don't leave me.'

'Shh,' Mary urged, 'They'll hear you. Anyway, we can still see each other.'

Elizabeth shook her head. 'If you marry him, that's it. I can't stand to watch you throw your life away.'

Mary's voice was shaking now but she had made up her mind. 'I'm sorry you feel that way.'

8

PREPARATIONS

Mother Pannell's Hut, West Yorkshire, 1560

Mother Pannell handed Mary a cup of herbal tea with loose leaves floating around in it. 'Here, drink this. It calms the nerves.'

'Thank you.' It smelt strong and fresh, but not pleasant. She sipped it anyway.

'What do you need, my child?'

Mary hesitated. 'Is Elizabeth here?'

She shook her head. 'She'll be working all day. I don't expect her home until dark.'

'Good.'

Mother Pannell busied herself organising her small glass bottles on the shelves of her hut, waiting for Mary to talk.

Mary put down her drink and warmed her hands by the fire. 'I wanted to ask you about—'

'Go on.'

'About pregnancy.'

'You are with child?'

Mary shook her head. 'No.'

Mother Pannell frowned. 'How long is it since you've been married?'

'It's been months. I can't help but think there's something wrong with me.'

She put a hand up to stop her talking. 'No. I won't have any of that. You're still young, and you haven't been married long.'

'I remember once you said something about the timing. I mean, there's a particular day that's best to lie with your husband.'

'Yes.' She sat next to Mary on the ground in front of the fire. 'Two weeks after you get your blood is the best time.'

'Two weeks,' Mary repeated, as if trying to memorise the phrase. 'What else?'

'Well, you should be taking care of yourself. Try not to worry too much about getting pregnant—it will happen when it happens. Don't drink too much, don't over-exert yourself and make sure you're getting enough sleep.'

Mary sighed. 'Is there nothing else I can do? I do so want to be a mother. This is the whole reason I got married in the first place.'

Mother Pannell took a deep breath. 'I know how you feel.'

'I don't think you do.'

She held her hand. 'I was never able to have a child of my own. I was married for years and years but it just never happened for me. I was devastated, but I got through it.'

'Why would you tell me that?' Mary shouted, pushing her hand away and standing up. 'I will have children. I'm not like you.'

Mother Pannell sighed. 'Of course. Just let me help you.'

'You just told me there was nothing you could do! Other than telling me to get some sleep, what good are you?'

'Mary! That is no way to speak to me,' Mother Pannell shouted.

Mary was silent. She had never heard her raise her voice before.

'Look, you have a lot of options. But some of them can be risky. It's best we do this slowly, if you are to have the best chance of conception with the least risk of complications.'

Mary supposed that made sense. 'But what am I to do in the meantime? I'm going mad, sitting in that empty house all day while John's at work.'

'What would you like to do?'

'As odd as it sounds, I miss being the Chapmans' maid. It was hard work and it's not that I really want to go back, but I like being busy.'

'What does John have to say about this? Would he allow you to work?'

Mary shrugged. 'I don't think he cares about me one way or the other.'

'Good. Then you'll work with me.'

Mary's face brightened. 'With you? Here?'

'Yes. You do want to, don't you?'

'I do. But what about Elizabeth? I don't want to run into her all the time.'

'Don't worry, she's not here during the day. Elizabeth never took any interest in my work, but I would like to pass it on to someone. If you have the inclination, I'd like to teach you. It would be good for you, I think, to have a basic knowledge of herbs and remedies. Especially if you plan on becoming a mother one day. After all, I won't be around forever.'

'Thank you, Mother Pannell. Really, thank you.'

9

MOTHERHOOD

Mary and John's House, West Yorkshire, 1575

With all her might, Mary pushed.

'Now breathe,' Mother Pannell urged. She demonstrated lots of quick outbreaths. 'That's it, just like that. Almost there.'

'I can't. I'm too tired, it's too hard,' Mary sighed. Sweat was dripping down her face and her sheets were drenched. She couldn't keep going any longer.

'One last push, Mary. Now.'

She pushed.

The baby started crying straight away and a wave of relief washed over Mary. She shut her eyes and let the sound of her child, alive and well, be the only thought in her mind. It was over. She held out her arms to hold the baby, but Mother Pannell pushed them back down onto the bed.

'Almost there. I'll just clean her up for you and then you can hold her.'

Her. Mary repeated the word in her mind. She had another daughter. Words couldn't describe the joy she felt. Her heart felt light, her body felt strong. How was it that she had brought another person into the world?

The rest of the day passed in the same state of happiness, and it wasn't until the evening that Mary remembered the reality of her situation. Mother Pannell had cleaned up and gone, and left Mary holding her new-born daughter to her chest. Her six-year-old daughter sat next to them in bed, walking her doll up and down Mary's arm.

The door to the house slammed shut as John returned home.

'Bess, sweetie, go to your room and play,' Mary said. 'Stay there until I come and get you.'

'But—'

'Now.'

She skipped into the other room. Mary held Agnes close to her chest and held her breath, ready to break the news to her husband.

'Another girl?' John shouted. 'We've been married—how long?'

'Sixteen years.'

'We've been married for sixteen years and you still haven't managed to give birth to a healthy son?'

Mary's eyes watered. Their first child had been a boy, but he had died the same day he was born. 'Please, don't shout,' she begged him.

He paced the room a few times before asking, 'the girl, is it healthy?'

Mary nodded eagerly.

He cursed under his breath. 'Do you expect me to believe all this is a coincidence?'

'What do you mean?' Mary asked in a shaky voice.

'The one boy you gave me died, but you manage to bring two perfectly healthy girls into the world. This is Mother Pannell's doing, isn't it? She's given you some mixture, some tonic, that means you only have daughters? She always did hate men.'

Mary shook her head. 'Why would I—no! Of course not.'

'I don't believe you.'

He stormed towards Mary and for a terrifying moment she thought he was going to raise a hand to their baby. She tucked her into the bedsheet next to her.

John hesitated. 'What was that?'

'Nothing,' Mary said quickly.

'You thought I was going to hurt her, didn't you?'

Mary's eyes widened. She tried to run through the possible answers in her mind, searching for the one he would find the least offensive.

'You are unbelievable. Do you really think I would hurt my own child?'

'No, of course not.'

'What kind of mother are you? What kind of wife?' He shook his head, in mock disbelief.

'Come here.'

'I'm supposed to stay in bed.'

He gritted his teeth. 'Come into the other room with me. Now.'

10

WOUNDED

John slammed the door shut behind him and Mary let out a wave of tears. How could her own husband treat her this way? What had she done to deserve this treatment from him?

Mary sniffed. Her head throbbed in pain and she knew she needed help. The pouring of the rain outside was deafening.

The shuffling of Bess's feet from the doorway pulled Mary from her stupor.

'Mother?' She whispered.

Mary's face was wet with tears. She blinked a couple of times and dabbed her face with a piece of her skirt. She turned to face Bess, whose lip was wobbling. 'Come here.' She held out her arms.

Bess wrapped her arms around her mother. 'Is he gone?'

'For now.' She squeezed her tightly until her sobs subsided.

Agnes started to cry in the other room.

Mary sighed. 'Now, let's go and see to your baby sister, shall we?'

Bess didn't let go of her mother as she struggled to stand up.

Mary put her firmly down but allowed her to hold her hand. 'Be a brave girl for me now.'

Bess nodded.

They crossed the room to where Agnes lay. With only one

hand available, Mary reached out to stroke her soft head. She whimpered. The baby stopped crying.

'There. That was all you needed, wasn't it?'

Her older daughter pulled on her arm.

'What is it, Bess?'

'Your face. It looks strange.'

She snatched her hand up and used both to feel the outline of her face. 'Yes. Yes, I'm sure it does. No matter, we shall go and see Mother Pannell.'

Mary grabbed a wet cloth and wiped her face as clean as she could. Then she pulled on her cap, pulling it down so that it covered most of her face. Bess kept her eyes on her teary mother.

'I'm fine. You're not worried about me, are you?'

Bess shook her head.

'Good.' She sniffed one more time before dressing herself and wrapping up her daughters warmly. Then she scooped up the baby who rested on her hip, and with the other hand grabbed a lantern and placed a lit candle inside. It would be shielded from the rain so they could find their way.

Mary kept her gaze down but Kippax was such a small town that she was likely to run into someone she knew. She only hoped that in this rain, most people would stay inside, warming themselves in front of a fire. Mary and the girls headed out of the centre of Kippax, following the path that led to the Lin Dike River.

'Stay close!' She called to Bess who was ahead, walking and splashing in the muddiest puddles along the path. The rain didn't bother her.

They didn't see anybody on the walk, and Bess walked all the way without needing Mary to carry her, so Mary was grateful. Eventually the outline of a hut emerged in the darkness. The doorway emitted a light from her fire. Mary cleared her throat when she got there and knocked.

'Mother Pannell?'

'Who is it?'

'Mary.'

'In!' She called.

Mary pushed open the door and stepped into the small space.

She motioned with the lantern for Bess to go inside, and she reluctantly followed.

'Say hello to Mother Pannell, Bess.'

'Hello Mother Pannell.' Bess stared at the floor, fidgeting with her fingers. She looked up at her mother. 'How long do we have to stay?'

'Bess! Go and sit down. And apologise to Mother Pannell for your rudeness.'

Bess never liked coming to see Mother Pannell—her hut was cold and always smelt of some new remedy she was brewing. But the main reason was that Mary was always too busy chatting to spend any time with Bess. It was boring.

'Sorry Mother Pannell.' She went over to the chickens, lay down on her stomach and started to poke them.

'What a dreadful sight.' Mother Pannell scowled at Mary. 'Put the baby there. Hand me that lantern. Let me look at you.'

She did as she was told.

'Right. This is going to sting. Bite this.' She handed her a rag. Mother Pannell walked over to a shelf full of small bottles and mixed the contents together in a separate bowl. She smeared the salve on Mary's face.

Mary screams were muffled by the rag, but Bess stared, eyes watering, all the same. Agnes began to cry again.

'You're lucky your nose is not broken. You could have been permanently disfigured.'

Mary groaned again.

'Even so, this will take time to heal.' She pulled off Mary's cloak and frowned. 'You have more wounds under here. I'll need you to undress.'

She spat out the rag and peeled off her clothes, damp with blood. Mother Pannell patched up her arm, her thigh and ankle with some rags after smearing them with the same salve she had applied to her face.

'There.' She started to put away her supplies—the medicines and bandages. It was crowded in this tiny hut with all of them inside.

'Bess.' She spoke to her daughter who had watched the whole

process, wide-eyed. 'I need to get dressed and speak to Mother Pannell for a little while. Why don't you put on your cloak and go and play by the river?'

When she had gone, Mary pulled on her bloody clothes and sighed. 'This is too much. I cannot handle this for much longer.'

Mother Pannell now sat by the fire, warming her hands. 'What do you mean by that?'

Mary raised her voice. 'Look at me! Look what he has done to me!' She picked up Agnes and joined Mother Pannell by the fire.

'I've seen worse.' Mother Pannell shrugged.

'I don't care! This has been going on for years. Soon he'll become violent towards the girls. I know it.'

'Men have violence in them,' Mother Pannell shrugged.

'He never used to hurt me, you know.' Mary's voice was lower now, but hoarse from shouting at her husband and at Mother Pannell.

'When did it start?'

'When William and Ellen got married and moved away, he got worse. It was like he saw how alone I was and took advantage. He always knows when I'm at my weakest.'

Mother Pannell nodded.

'He got angry whenever I lost a baby. He blamed me.' Mary remembered every pregnancy. She was not a lucky woman; her body had struggled every time she had tried to bear a child.

'It's always too easy to blame the woman.'

'But I did everything right. There was nothing I could have done. He should have known that.'

She shook her head. 'Men will do anything to pass the blame onto someone other than themselves.'

Mary touched the bandage on her arm and flinched.

'Is it too tight?'

'No. It's fine.' Mary said.

'You'll manage. Anyway, can't he be happy with the girls you've given him? That's more than a lot of people get.' Mother Pannell took a gulp of a drink she had poured earlier and poured one for Mary.

Mary gulped it down. 'Well, he is, mostly. But it's not just that which worries me.'

'What is it?'

'He's started talking about witchcraft again.'

'What do you mean?'

'He thinks I've been working with you. Working on some way to have only daughters, not sons. That's why he blames me so strongly this time.'

'That's a serious accusation.'

'It's bad. I think he might do something.'

'You mean hurt the girls?'

'Yes. Or worse.' She lowered her voice. 'I don't want Bess to hear me.'

Mother Pannell nodded and leaned in. 'What is it you want from me?'

'I want him gone.' Mary's voice was deep, serious.

Mother Pannell drew a sharp breath.

'I'll do anything.'

'This talk isn't right.' She shook her head. 'You should not speak of these things.'

'Please. Mother Pannell, please help me. I have nobody else to turn to.' Tears welled up in her eyes. 'I need to protect my children.'

Mother Pannell paused. 'How serious are you about this?' She whispered.

'Completely. I have wanted this for a long time.' Mary said.

She sat up and walked away from the fire to where she kept her remedies. Hidden underneath a pile of old rags was a large bottle. She poured a couple of drops into a smaller bottle and pushed a cork into the top. 'Take this.'

Mary's heartbeat quickened. 'I am to put this in his drink?'

'Yes.' Mother Pannell had already busied herself by tidying up the hut.

'How long will it take?' Mary still couldn't believe she was here. She finally had the upper hand against her husband. Before she got married, she never would have thought herself capable of murder. But here and now, it was a different story. She found herself anxious, excited.

'Not long.'

A noise sounded outside the hut. It made Mary jump. She grabbed the bottle before Elizabeth entered, holding Bess's hand. There was very little space inside so Elizabeth was pressed up against Mary.

'Good evening, Mother Pannell.' She nodded in greeting and Bess rushed over to hug her mother. 'I didn't know you were expecting company—am I disturbing you?'

Elizabeth widened her eyes in concern at Mary's blood-stained cloak, and pulled her messy, light-brown hair out of her cap. She shook it free and pushed past Mary to sit down next to the fire.

Mary avoided Elizabeth's gaze. 'Good evening. I was just leaving. Thank you again, Mother Pannell. For—for tending to my wounds.'

11

OPPORTUNITIES

Mary hurried off, hiding her bloody face. She didn't want Elizabeth to see her like this, after all this time. Elizabeth's voice called after her. 'Mary! Mary, wait!'

Her heart jumped. Elizabeth's voice was exactly the sound she needed to hear. She stopped walking and waited. Elizabeth put her hand on Mary's shoulder. Mary closed her eyes and turned to face her. Elizabeth's eyes were only dimly lit by the lantern light, but they had the same brightness they always did. She was lost for words.

Elizabeth held her hand to Mary's cheek. 'Your face—this was him, wasn't it? John?'

Mary bit her lip.

'He can't keep treating you like this.'

'It's not that simple.'

Elizabeth scoffed. 'He's not going to stop.'

'I know.'

'You have to do something!'

Mary hesitated. 'I can't.'

Elizabeth raised her eyebrows. 'I heard you talking to Mother Pannell.'

'I—I just—it's not what you think—'

She shook her head. 'I don't care about him. Do what you need to do.'

'It's not about me,' Mary said quickly. 'I can handle him. But I'm just scared for my girls.'

'You don't need to explain. If you need my help—'

'No. I won't drag you into this.'

'Are you sure you can do this?'

Mary sighed. 'I don't know. I'm not a murderer.'

'It's not murder. Not when your life is in danger.'

'He would never hurt me that badly,' Mary insisted.

'And your girls?'

Mary didn't say anything.

Elizabeth sighed. 'Whatever happens, don't hesitate. He deserves to die. Just promise me you'll have a backup plan. If he found out what you were planning—'

Mary nodded. 'I know. He won't. I promise.'

Elizabeth took her hand and pressed it to her lips. 'Follow me.'

'Bess! Come this way,' Mary called.

Elizabeth took Mary's hand and led her along the river to a second, bigger hut that Mary hadn't seen before.

'What's this?'

Elizabeth grinned. 'It's ours. I built it for us.'

Mary gasped. 'What do you mean?'

'Exactly that. We can be together here. It's our own space, where we have plenty of privacy. No one from Kippax ever comes out here, unless it's to see Mother Pannell. And even then, they come at night and don't ask questions.'

Mary shook her head. 'No, this is crazy. We've barely spoken in years. You can't just build us a house and expect me to move in! I have a life. A husband, children.'

Elizabeth leaned her head to one side. 'You don't love him. I know you don't.'

'This is crazy,' Mary repeated, though she was grinning too now.

'Tell me you don't love me, and I'll stop. Tell me you don't want this and I won't pester you again.' Elizabeth took a deep breath.

'But if any part of you is excited about this—if part of you wants to build a life here with me—'

Mary squeezed her hand. 'My children—'

Elizabeth pushed open the door and gestured to the space. 'There's room for them, too. For all of us.'

Mary hesitated.

'I know you're worried about leaving your husband. But don't be. He's a problem we can solve.'

12

DEFEATED

Her heart racing, Mary stirred the pot. The glass bottle felt heavy in her pocket. Could she really do this? Had her husband truly been terrible enough that he deserved to die? Even if he did, was Mary a murderer? She tried to keep her breath steady, even as John's footsteps sounded in the kitchen.

'Dinner ready yet?' John grunted.

'Almost,' Mary said. She hoped her voice sounded more confident than she felt. Elizabeth's voice sounded in her mind: promise me you'll have a backup plan. What if this didn't work?

John snapped at her, 'what's the matter with you?'

She froze. 'I—I'm just tired.'

He frowned but left the room anyway. 'I'll just get changed.'

Mary exhaled. She took the small bottle out of her cloak and stared at the few drops inside. They were clear, like water. For all anyone else knew, it was harmless. But she knew better. Mary dished out a plate of tomato stew for Bess before giving herself a larger portion, and finally she emptied the bottle into the pot and stirred it around thoroughly before spooning the rest onto John's plate. She carried the plates over to the table. 'Food's ready!' Her breathing quickened, but desperate not to let her anxiety show, she sat down.

'Mother?' Bess asked.

'Not now,' Mary snapped. She looked around, searching for something, anything, that she might be able to keep close, just in case. She reached for a knife, but Bess started crying, and Agnes copied her.

'Stop it, girls. Wait for your father, and then you can eat.' She held Agnes to her chest to feed her. 'Shh.'

John came in, swigging something from a bottle. He slumped himself down at the table.

Mary cursed under her breath. She couldn't take the knife now. She joined the others and tucked into her stew.

Bess reached a hand over to her father's plate, grabbed a handful and almost put it in her mouth.

'Bess!' Mary shouted. She pushed the table away and leaned right over towards her and slapped her hand away. She started to cry again.

John stared at his wife, wide-eyed. 'What are you doing?'

Mary's eyes widened. 'Nothing, it's just—Bess, stop crying. It's rude to eat off somebody else's plate. Your food is in front of you. Now, eat up.'

John didn't touch his food. His eyes flitted over to the kitchen area, where the small glass bottle, now empty, lay next to the cooking pot.

Mary swallowed. 'Shh, Bess.'

'Come here, Bess. I don't mind. Why don't you try some of mine?' John asked.

Mary glared at Bess. 'Eat your own.' Mary gulped down hers.

'Mary! Stop it. Bess, try some of mine.' He pushed his plate towards her.

Bess was silent. She just sat there, watching her parents.

'Don't,' Mary said.

'I knew it.' He picked up his plate and threw it at the wall, smearing it with tomato sauce and small pieces of meat.

'Bess!' Mary shouted, 'Go outside and play, now.'

Bess ran outside.

'Do you think I'm stupid?' John asked. 'I know exactly what you just tried to do to me.'

Mary shook her head, as if that would solve anything. 'It was

46

nothing—I didn't do anything.' But it was too late. Elizabeth was right. Mary should have thought of a backup plan. She racked her brains trying to think of something.

'I could turn you in right now.'

She held Agnes close to her, wishing with all she had that he wouldn't hurt them.

'Do you know what the penalty is? For trying to kill your husband? For petty treason?'

Mary shook her head.

'They'll burn you,' he laughed. 'They'll burn your body and invite all of Kippax to watch—including your precious girls.'

'No!' How could he threaten her with this? Being burned alive? A dark thought entered her mind, but she shook it off.

He laughed again.

'Please, no. Don't turn me in,' she begged. 'I'll do anything. My girls should never have to see that. Please, John. If you ever loved me, don't do this.'

He slumped back in his chair and stroked his beard. 'Well, I have one other idea, but I don't know if you'll agree.'

'I will. Please, John. Just don't take my girls from me.'

He ordered her to pack their bags. She was not to say goodbye to Mother Pannell or Elizabeth, or even to any of their neighbours. He told her she couldn't have any contact with her father or siblings. They left on foot that night, late enough that they wouldn't run into anyone on the way. They arrived at a tiny wooden shed with holes in the roof. The rain came through in drips, so Mary set out some pots to collect the water.

'How long will we be staying here?' Mary pulled Agnes close, hoping she would be able to get through the nights in this place.

'We'll be here until I'm sure I can trust you. I won't be married to a witch, and if you do anything to make me suspect you're continuing on with this—this stupidity—I'll turn you in.'

13

FIRE

Mary and John's Hut, West Yorkshire, 1575

After being stuck in this shed for almost a week, Mary was ready to give up. Her only company was her two young daughters. John hadn't been here since the first night, but Mary was too scared to leave. She bounced Agnes on her hip, trying to calm her the best she could. 'Shh. I'm here.'

But Agnes wouldn't stop crying.

'Shall we go for a walk?' John had been clear. She was not to leave this place. But he wasn't around anyway, and if she stayed inside for one more day, she was sure she would be driven mad. Mary held out a hand for Bess and she took it.

Out in the sun, Mary looked one way, and then the other. As far as she could see, there was nobody around. She couldn't even hear anyone. Where had John taken them? They were surrounded by fields, empty even of animals. If he planned to hurt them, no one would hear their screams. The thought made her shiver. 'Come on, let's go for a quick walk, then back home.'

'Mother?' Bess asked.

'Yes?'

'When can we go home?'

Mary sighed. Bess remembered as well as she did that this

wasn't really their home. But there was nothing she could say to make her feel better, so they walked in silence.

Once they got near to Mother Pannell's house, Mary rested Agnes on the ground. 'Stay with your sister,' she told Bess.

She crept up to the door, pushed it open and shook Elizabeth awake. She groaned loudly.

'Shh!' Mary urged.

Elizabeth blinked a few times before her face filled with worry. 'What's wrong?'

'Come for a walk with me.'

She reached for her cloak and followed her outside. They took the girls back towards the shed and left them outside, on a soft patch of grass. Mary didn't answer any questions until they got back.

She led Elizabeth inside. 'I've missed you,' she whispered.

Elizabeth wrapped her arms around her. 'What happened? What is this place?'

'Just be with me,' Mary said.

They lay back on the pile of straw Mary had been sleeping on. Elizabeth kissed her softly, then harder. It must have been an hour before a man pushed open the door, holding Agnes and with Bess cowering behind him.

'John!' Mary's eyes widened. She wrapped her dress around herself, but it was too late.

'Leave,' he said to Elizabeth.

Elizabeth whispered, 'I won't go far. If he hurts you, scream, and I'll come back.'

'I said, leave!' John shouted.

She hurried out.

Mary pulled her dress over her head and took Agnes from her husband, then motioned for Bess to sit next to her.

John spoke in a raspy voice that made Mary shiver. 'I told you not to see her anymore.'

'I'm sorry,' Mary kept her eyes down. 'But I was going mad, stuck in here.'

'You're supposed to be my wife!'

Mary mumbled, 'I am.'

'I can't trust you anymore.'

'John, please.'

He grabbed Bess. 'Do you know what your mother was doing, while you were outside playing?'

She looked at her mother, terrified.

'Don't touch her!' Mary screamed.

He threw Bess back on the mound of hay where she slept and she sobbed. Mary wrapped her arms around her and Agnes.

'You disgust me,' he said, slurring his words. 'I'm going to sleep.'

Mary did not sleep. She kept her eyes open until she heard John's snoring. With or without Mother Pannell's help, Mary was determined to get rid of her husband.

She waited at least an hour before stirring, to make sure John was in a deep sleep. She did not want him waking up.

While moving as little as possible, she pushed herself up to standing and collected in a bag the things she needed from the kitchen: lettuce, vinegar, bryony root, a large pot and she also took the piece of flint from by the fireplace. She reached down to pick up Agnes as slowly as possible. She stroked her forehead just how she liked it, and thankfully she didn't wake up. Then she slid a hand into Bess's and pulled to get her to stand up. Bess moaned gently so Mary quickly held a finger up to her lips. 'Shh,' she whispered. In her half-asleep state, Bess did seem to understand, and followed Mary outside into the cold.

Mary took them back to the tree and gently placed Agnes on the ground. She was still sleeping. 'Stay here, both of you, you hear me?'

Bess nodded.

She put the bag of ingredients next to them before adding, 'don't touch these.'

Henbane had always grown in Kippax, so it wasn't long before she found some of the small yellow flowers, visible by the light of the moon. As quickly as she could, she mixed the ingredients in the pan and lit a fire to boil them. Bess was sitting next to Agnes, leaning against the tree. Mary prayed they wouldn't make any noise. When the mixture was finally ready, she crept back to the shed and poured it into John's open mouth as he snored. He stirred and almost choked on it, but swallowed it down without waking up.

Mary ran to the woods surrounding them and collected as many dry logs as she could, and she would use the rushes inside the shed as kindling. Until now, she wasn't sure if she could really do it. Not until he raised a hand to Bess. That made her decision easy.

She laid out the sticks by the bed where John slept, making sure to block the doorway, just in case he did wake up. She flicked the flint onto the rushes. Nothing. She kept going until she saw a spark. Finally it caught alight. She leaned down to blow on the fire. It didn't take long for it to grow. Mary closed her eyes and held her arm in the fire for an agonising couple of seconds. Then she kicked the rushes over so that they blocked the doorway and hurried away, back to the tree.

Mary stood with her daughters and watched. The shed was made of wood, and it wasn't long before the whole thing was up in flames. John didn't make a sound—Mary was glad. She wanted him gone, but she could never burn someone alive. She was so grateful to Mother Pannell for showing her how to make dwale, and to Elizabeth for making her see that this was the best thing to do for her family. The brightness of the flames was blinding. 'Come on girls, let's go.'

'Mother,' Bess said, pulling on her skirts.

'I said, come on, Bess. It's time for us to go.'

'Mother, look! It's Father!'

Horrified, Mary squinted into the light of the fire and saw the outline of a man, too badly wounded to scream, burning alive.

14

LIFE

Bess looked up her mother and sobbed.

'We're safe now,' Mary said, her eyes welling up with tears. 'He can't hurt you now.' She kissed the top of her head. 'I love you; you know that don't you? One day, I'll explain all this to you.'

Bess cried more loudly.

'Shh, please. Let's go home, back to Kippax.' Mary followed the path, which eventually led them to a fork in the road—the way to Mother Pannell's—and to Elizabeth's. 'Let's go this way,' Mary said with a deep breath. She had to see Elizabeth.

Her heart was pounding all the way there, not sure how much she should tell her. When they passed Mother Pannell's hut, Elizabeth's voice was clear inside. 'She's here,' Mary whispered.

With her right arm badly burned, she was holding Agnes in her left arm. 'Bess, can you knock for me?'

'Who is it?' Mother Pannell called.

Mary hesitated before calling back, 'it's me.'

Elizabeth's footsteps raced to the door and her eyes widened in alarm at Mary's appearance. 'What happened?' She wrapped her arms tightly around her and Mary let her for a while before she groaned in pain.

'I'm sorry—my arm. It hurts.'

'Bring her inside,' Mother Pannell said. 'I'll bandage you up.'

She rattled around her shelves for something to wrap around her arm.

'There was a fire—'

'Are the children alright?' Elizabeth asked, looking from Bess to Agnes.

'Yes, they're fine.'

'And John?'

Mary hesitated.

'How's John?' Elizabeth asked again.

'He's dead.'

Mother Pannell froze. 'Dead? Are you sure?'

Mary nodded. 'There was a terrible accident.'

'Oh, Mary!' Elizabeth hugged her again.

Mother Pannell caught Mary's eye—she understood.

'What are you going to do now?' Elizabeth asked.

'I was hoping to talk to you about that, actually. We need somewhere to live.'

Elizabeth's face brightened. 'You mean—you want to come and live with me?'

Mary grinned. 'If the offer's still there.'

'Of course!'

Mother Pannell cleared her throat. 'Don't go getting ahead of yourself. Yes, you can live over in Elizabeth's hut, and I can give you some work here—I know you're good with remedies, but that won't be enough.'

'What do you mean?' Mary asked.

'Your husband used to bring in enough money to support your whole family, but now it's on you to support two young children. It's no easy feat, especially for a woman on her own.'

Mary bit her lip. She hadn't thought about that.

'If you're interested, the housemaid position has just opened up at the Withams' place—Ledston Hall.'

LIKED THIS BOOK?

CONNECT WITH ME!

I love hearing what readers have to say about my books so please leave me a review.

As an indie author, reviews are really helpful for me. Thank you so much for all your support!

For more about the English Witch Trials, you can read the articles on my website:

melissamanners.com

Read the prequel, **Becoming The Pannell Witch**, available now.

To be the first to hear about my next book,
The Witham Witch, sign up to my mailing list on my website.

I really love to hear from my readers, so follow me:

facebook.com/melissamannerswrites

twitter.com/melissamanners

instagram.com/melissamannerswrites

amazon.com/author/melissamanners

goodreads.com/melissamanners

ABOUT THE AUTHOR

Melissa was born and raised in London where her book obsession began. She would take a book everywhere she went (she still does this, and probably always will). Her writing career started at the tender age of eight when she wrote her first 'book': a folded booklet summarising the story of Persephone.

Her love of Greek mythology continued into adulthood, as did her love of storytelling. She spent her teen years writing angst-ridden fanfic until she found NaNoWriMo, which she entered year after year.

It was not until she was in her twenties that she found her love of historical fiction. The historical period that most stuck out was that of the English Witch Trials—horrifying, yet fascinating. The treatment of women in particular (but also a range of other people seen as 'different'), is what Melissa wanted to address in her own writing.

She loves to reframe the narrative that has been passed down to us, mostly by men, and allow stories to be told from a new perspective. It's a shame we don't have many records from this period, but through historical fiction we can give those neglected members of society a voice.

Printed in Great Britain
by Amazon

30052871R00037